RAILROAD

JENNY FOOTLE

MANDOLIN PUBLISHING

Published by the Mandolin Publishing Group
For more information, write to:
mandolinpublishing@gmail.com
Or find us on Facebook
https://www.facebook.com/Mandolinpublishing
Copyright © Jenny Footle, 2023
Cover design layout © Amanda Blackwood, 2023

The writing within this book is based on the author's personal experiences over a period of many years and is not the advice of a medical expert. Some names and characteristics of people mentioned have been changed, some events have been compressed.

DEDICATED

To those who took the time to see me, and didn't let me disappear.

To my Savior who whispered, "I've got you" and still has my heart.

TABLE OF CONTENTS

CHAPTER ONE:

THE EARLY YEARS

SECRETS OF LIFE

People are forests
With many hidden beauties.
Few people seek to venture in,
Through the thick, dark air,
Past the pillars that surround
With harsh bark and whistling leaves,
And into the spring of their life
Where the buzzing insects play
Passing the secrets within.

YELLOW

I Am Yellow
I am a shade of white
And a tone of Brown.
I go well with black,
But that's not who I am.
I Am Yellow.

I am Yellow

I am the rays of the sun
That shine upon the world
And touch everything,
But I am not part of the world.
I Am Yellow.

I Am Yellow
I am bright and happy
I highlight the important and unnoticed
And make them stand out.
I can be what you're looking for,
But I am not what you seek.
I Am Yellow

I Am Yellow
Where darkness does not thrive
And nothing will be cold for long.
I can warm your heart or be your shining star,
Your little sunshine or your burning flame.
But I could never be you,
I Am Yellow

BECAUSE I SEE

Dear Eyes,
I forgive you for all the secrets you told,
    Because you made them believe more lies.
I forgive you for tearing down so many walls,
    Because you salvage the good bricks for a new one.
I forgive you for letting them in,
    Because they get trapped.
I forgive you for getting them lost,
    Because it distracts the weak wanderers.
I forgive you for the flood,
    Because everything is lost downstream.
I forgive you for wandering off,
    Because I would have never seen it coming.
I forgive you for scaring me,
    Because you never touched me.
I forgive you for closing,
    Because it gave me time to escape.
I forgive you for all these things,
    Because you have shown me this beautiful sight called life.

HANDS-ON

I see all the pictures you created,
All the letters you wrote, all the bad ideas you crunched.
Look at all the things you sculpted and carved,
The things you built, what you destroyed.
I feel the fists you made,
They may have felt the ground, but never a face.

You landed on many shoulders and in many hands,
Your grip is tight, but you push away hindrances.
I hear the praise you give,
The hollow doors you knocked on, bones you popped.
Listen to the rhythm you beat out,
Hear the tapping, hear the scratching.
Sometimes you are right, but you are never wrong.
Sometimes you are left, but never are you forgotten.
Your reputation is mysteriously well-known.
From being "caught red-handed"
To "lending a helping hand."
They know you "had a hand in it" somewhere.
Feel all the futures you touched, fingerprints you left, lives you
held – don't let go.

THAT UPSIDE DOWN SMILE

It's that little quirky grin
That arises when I giggle
And it really is a smile,
But it bows down more than up.
I think it's momma's way
Of pointing to heaven

It is a gentle smile
Showing a calm interest
In whatever happened to spark it.
One of those expressions that screams;
I love you, you make me smile.
And oh the satisfaction I get
When I know it was me who caused it.

It's hard to bring that smile out
Like a true laugh,
You can't get it to come on cue.
Funny how it taunts you
When trying to capture it on camera
It escapes like someone jumping around,
They just keep coming in and out of view
But magically it's never there when you snap the shot.

You have to catch it at that perfect moment
And embrace the time while it lasts.
Before you know it, that upside down smile can change
Disappearing into a normal grin
Going back to the normal grind
The kind of smile everyone wears when they show happiness
The sort of smile that bows up
And points straight to the heart.

BREATHING ENCLOSURE

As booming rays parch the surrounding space
Only a few sparkle through the tightly stacked trees
Exposing crevices of bark.
Beasts are bewildered
As their fur is warmed and
Glowing they venture
Past the pillars that surround
With thick, cold, ancient marble
And into the fountain forested over
Where the buzzing insects play
Passing the secrets.

THE FALL UPWARD

Love is up in the air
        but I am reaching.
My hopes are high
        but the sun is blinding.
I wish
        but the star has fallen.
Joy is deep
        but the bottom is dark.
Mountains are tall
        yet the rain falls down.
The wind blows hard
        and my feet haven't left the ground.
You look at me
        and I turn away.
I see them
        but not the same way.
Your image is distorted
        from here under water.
My life is diluted
        as I wait here drowning.
Shriveled hands
        slip from help.
I'm sure they are pretty from another perspective
        but the water makes you waiver
And waving I am,
        Goodbye.

THE FALL UPWARD TOO

Pleasant conversations of exciting news and achievements
      but your clenched jaw
Probably incinerates your teeth when you turn my way
      even though you brought me.

It's getting too hot
      And going out to the dock
You rupture, but it won't be on me
      Just on my hand
As a glide of my palm to your chest
      Will help you cool off.

Your image is distorted
      from being under water.
Your life is diluting
      as I watch you drowning.
Just staring, not grinning
      we hold the same glare
Until you accuse me,
      I made you do it.
I tried, but did I?
      No more holding on.

Shriveled hands
      slip from help.
I'm sure they are pretty from another perspective
      but the water makes you waiver
And waving I am,
      Goodbye.

GET IT TO GO

Do you remember?
I remember.
I remember the first time I heard someone sing in the car.
I remember the first time I saw a robin's egg blue.
I remember all those years I tolerated hearing, "you wouldn't understand."
I remember the first time I saw a boy dance.
I remember the words, "Let's play a game."
I remember the first time I was turned away for being female.
I remember pushing him out of that tree.
I remember the only time I talked back to mother, I still don't know if I'm sorry.
I remember getting a 0%, because I wasn't fast enough.
I remember the 50% test, and the 0% when I tried again.
I remember making it through a whole day without anyone seeing my tears, when I held them in.
I remember putting a hole in the window with a bullet.
I remember the taste of grape.
I remember jumping, falling, swimming.
       But not breathing or hitting the surface.
I remember when He talked to me.
I remember 15 minutes.

It was unreal reality.
       What do you remember?

I don't remember the first time my father hit me.
I don't remember making any promises.
I don't remember the last time we talked.
I don't remember hearing the word, "enough"
I don't remember what really happened.
I don't remember where I've run.

I don't remember saying that.
I forget when you ask me to, mostly.

UNEASY

Another friend has passed me
By as if I were
Concealed. A camouflaged
Disguise, hope they don't see it in my
Eyes, or worse,
Find the bruises before they heal.

JENNIFER

I told you "I love you"
And you said "I love me too"
Which seemed selfish,
But I'm not sure I wanted your love in return.
Love that threatened to kill
Love that left scars
Love that ordered rum in high school so you felt like a pirate
Love that rebelled until it came down to it and then you were
fiercely
There for yourself,
Apologizing
But begging me to take the
Fall for your choices.
I did.
It didn't help you though,
Only you could help you, and you didn't.

You see I was experimenting with the phrase "I love you"
And it returned more than empty,
It returned by taking,
By needing but not giving
Betrayal not bonding.

And so I wouldn't try it out again for a while.
Years later I'd tell the person who cared "I love you"
And they paused -- "You never told me that before"
I was crushed
My beacon of hope
Kindness in human form
Just now hearing those words from me

I'm married now
Surely I've learned to use them

Surely I know their power
Surely I know what they mean.
But sometimes I guard them,
Only a select few, if I really mean it
But sometimes I throw them
Out into the universe
And see what comes my way.

JENNY FOOTLE

CHAPTER TWO:

NATIVE AMERICAN

TO CATCH THE RAIN, THERE IS EARTH

It never rains, so when it does, we celebrate
If the sky looks dull, or heavy
We dance the rain dance to the crash in a rain stick.
We played in the warm rain,
Kneaded the earth the next day with bare feet,
Covered each others' skin and hair
With the mud,
Ran through the streets knowing we'd be seen but not
recognized.
And after the sun took the rain from our earthy shells,
We washed it away and entertained new, soft skin.
There would still be dirt on us, later you would find it in the
oddest places,
But it is true, you can't wait for rain,
to wash away your dirt.
Those who wait will be seen, but not recognized.

SILENCE

My mind was so busy,
I would relax but then go in and out of listening for every little
sound my ears could pick up. Then I was singing "I Need You"
by Faith Hill in my head
Wondering if I always had background music.
My mind would go blank.
Then Rebecca saying how none of her clients wanted to be alone
with their thoughts.

Silence… it took me a while to hear the other noises.
I just kept having memories of making rain sticks
and living at the end of the trail,
and running with dream catchers…
and then peaceful stillness.

Silence,
that echoed off the walls.
The music lingered,
especially the drums -- invaded the silence.
Clearer thoughts, more images.

CLEO' S TEA

Only in Colorado do you get date rape drugged in a hot cup of
tea.
It would happen that the only dance you remember from your
own heritage
would be the one you freeze during while dancing it on stage
and you never go back.
It's too close to home,
It's too close to the heart.
While they scorn you as you dance their dance,
But when you lack the ability to dance your own dance,
That's when you hang up your spandex and go home.

That's when you move on and blend into the beige culture
That claims there's no culture --
We're all human and on our own path.
On our own.
On our.
On.

Move on.
Don't get stuck.
Only dreamers get stuck in something gone wrong.
Movers move on.

Is that right?
Is that what your tea bag said?

Shun dancing because we can't --
It's uncomfortable.
Embrace singing because we embrace the tongue --
Which cannot be tamed…
But you thought dancing was bad?
What leads to destruction…

I don't really care --
You do.

What revitalizes,
That's what I want.
I don't fear destruction,
I've already died.
Let's live, and live it right.

WHEN MY HEART SHUT DOWN

It wasn't shocking
It wasn't violent
If it were, there would be something to resist, something to fight
But there was no fight
No response
A nothingness. Emptiness? A void…
Avoided
They didn't speak to me,
They didn't look at me,
But they moved me. So deeply

Pure joy turned to calculated decision making.
Taking up space turned to shrinking back.
Endless adventure to too many decisions.

Like running through fields barefoot as fast as you want,
Creating little skips when your foot hits something unexpected
But it just propels you forward more.

To finding yourself on a sea of hardened concrete, suffocating
the earth,
Looking up at sky rises, feeling so small,

But not like before when you felt a part of it all,
Now your smallness is overwhelming, so alone…
Running would make you look crazy here
So you become unmovable, alone, small and insignificant
instead of delightful…
And here, definitely avoided.

So you close the doors
No need to flip the "Open" sign,
Just take it down.

No one will stop by long enough to see if you're in there.
But now you sit inside. And stare.
All the possibilities and joys you built up
Turn to burdens and things you have to find a new home for.
Maybe you'll just leave it all and walk away,
But that would be irresponsible.
So you sit.

People walk by but don't look in.
When they see you outside, they'll smile
But sitting
Here, inside,
you have obligations.
Not shocking, not forceful, and amidst everything you're sitting
in,
There is a nothingness. Emptiness? A void.

Your heart is just not in it anymore.
You have decisions to make, responsibilities, obligations,
Ways to operate out of considerations of others,
And a desire to avoid more pain
Stronger than a desire to feel more
Love and freedom.

HOW CAN IT BE

when the sky laughs at the birds that fly, instead of engulfing
them in all their greatness....
what have we become.
when all is lost, and they take more...
what have we become.
when the grass pricks the feet of a child, instead of softening
their step...
what have we become.
when we crucify the one who saves us, instead of dying for
him...
what have we become.

RUNNER

I'm a runner.
I run,
Often
It's in my blood
I used to run with my people
We cover more ground this way.
Showing up at the same place, same time, together.
United in strength, bravery, courage, and a commitment to our
lives.

We all run the same course, sometimes in our own strength,
sometimes as one.
The one coming from behind has to try extra hard,
And once they make it to the front, time to coast, that speed is
not meant to be maintained. Sometimes tempted to keep the fast
pace and make the whole group catch up,
Their job is actually to occasionally slow the whole group down,
So the next leader can rise from the end of the line.
The middle keeps the tempo, keeps the core strong,
chats to one another and cheers the one striving toward the front,
waiting their turn to end up at the back and strive ahead, but until
then, they keep steady.
And we take our turn, as we run together.

But now I only run with them in spirit,
Away from my people, away from others I thought were my
people
I run.
Away from the human world and deep into nature.
Spending more time with trees, feeling grounded on mountains
I run
Away from people, feeling safer in the forest than in a crowded
room

RAILROAD

I run

Away from the violence, when there seems to be no end
I ran
Away from reality, headlong into a nightmare.
I ran
Toward the temporary high, the space where for a moment, I
don't feel them
And I ran
From the disapproval of others, and the thoughts running through
my mind
I ran
From emotions, from the exhaustion in my body, the fear that I
might not be able to
Run away
From myself and the monsters in my head and in my closet.

Because when I stop
And pause
It rushes over me
Suddenly it's harder to breathe
I start to finally sweat
My body stops sending pain relief to my skinned knee
And I start to feel
Everything

Which leads me to run
Harder
Deeper into the forest

I run away from distractions, from the noise,
I run so fast I only hear the wind boxing my ears,
Focusing only on my breath
Not tripping on rocks,
Taking in the views when the path is smooth
Being grateful for all the beauty and life around me

While still running

Feeling the cool of the valley,
Never losing the wonder of wildflowers,
Leaning into the curves of the switchback
Falling into the down
To make it back up

I run.

Smiling at the birds as they dare you to look around,
Giggling at the obstacles that make you pick up your feet, jump
higher, run faster
Slowing down only to look Deer in the eye, not lingering in their
vulnerability, but acknowledging them and continuing on
respectfully
They have a place here too

And you must run on
Your spirit is full
And the people are waiting for you to get back
And share your life

WE KNOW

Don't call it judgment
Or not getting to know someone.
You don't have to disguise it as intuition,
It's called context clues.
Why is this person, these people,
Talking to you?
Why did they make the journey into this territory where they
don't belong,
Where even the Earth does not
Welcome their presence?
They want to get to know you…
To see you? Or see what you know?
"We knew you could talk" and
"See, that wasn't so bad"
Are insults on my humanity
Invasions on my personhood
It doesn't make me feel better
About your talking
Or make you less bad

I am quietly scheming
Keeping the peace is not loud
Restoring peace is loud, but I am avoiding
        Losing it
I don't need to confront you like you did to me
Your time will come, for now I will protect
What you thought would nourish you,
Our food, the land, our bodies
Will not

Our spices that will make you feel
The burning inside that is your soul
The Mother Earth cannot hide the

Pain you cause her
and her children,
If not her self,
will rise against you

Our bodies will not serve you,
And never truly satisfy you
Our souls will rise as you fall

Because I am quiet does not mean
That you will not be spoken to.
And your badness is not diminished
Because I am strong enough to survive it.

There is power in knowing
That we are one with the Earth
And abide in the One who is greater
My fight is not you one human
My peace is not lost to you
I know our true power
And you are no match
And it's not always my job,
Nor do you deserve to be told
By my voice, my beautiful voice
This ugly, defected, thing you have become.

RAILROAD

There's something about watching
Earth take back her body.
Witnessing the overgrowth on train tracks
Where an Other hammered into her
          Huge stakes
And laid iron chains
She could not break free from
So commerce could move across the landscape of her life more
quickly
Keep her down
Under the track

People stand back,
It's dangerous to even be near the flow of traffic
Going across her body
But if you attempt to sit with her, you might get crushed, overrun
by demand
The Other will come clean you off, brush you off of her
As she's tied down, unable to use her gifts
Of helping restore you to life, return you to dust
But there will be remnants of you, reminding her, of her strength
that she holds
And one day, she might break free.

She might finally cave under the weight and find that when she
lets go, the chains will break,
Maybe even in a landslide, if not a giant hole.
Or she might buckle, and erupt from all the friction and
disturbance,
Leaving a giant scar(e), but leaving nonetheless.

Or River of Life will come,
First in gentle rain, maybe in rushing torrent,

Flooding her heart, softening her hard outer shell that was
keeping the chains on the surface, Sinking the flow of "progress"
that beat her down for so long, like a Red Sea parting,
The flood that washes over and drowns out all the noise,
In what the other sees as a loss of their fabricated tool on top of
her life,
Earth finds peace,
Breath,
As everything is destroyed or covered by Water.

She waits for the rainbow.
The promise from Water that we can begin again, in a new way.
Earth soaks it all in, but the chains remain,
They no longer bind her
Life grows, overgrows, envelops them,

The wood and ties of her kind that were used to keep her down,
she will break down,
Return them to Earth, to herself, use them to nourish once again,
Return them to nature and the circle of life, instead of holding
their weight against them,
Earth forgives and reconciles slowly.

The iron will remain, the mark on her body and her mind, as she
pulls out the poisonous stakes.
One by one, focus on new growth, not just pulling out old pains.
It's a process.
In the meantime, she delights in children being free to delight in
her, despite the scars of the tracks,
And the teenagers who even come by to rip out parts of the iron,
she's thankful, and doesn't fret about the choices they'll make
with the same old metal, maybe they'll recycle it for something
good.
As the shrubs grow and the children play, the old paths are
forgotten, abandoned as no longer useful,

Earth focuses on the freedom after being abandoned,
The chance to do what she does best
Be.
Be the foundation of life
Reclaim her body
Facilitate growth
        and delight.

End Note:
Earth would like to take this opportunity to thank River,
For saving her, nurturing her, and returning her to Life. May she
never dread the tears of Sky, but welcome the grief, healing, and
chance to grow some more.

Afterward:
Many people dismiss the sex trade as the oldest profession and
others call it the oldest oppression. And just like industrialism
and how it destroys the planet, people dismiss it as progress.
When will we stop dismissing our Earth and our women as
collateral damage for forward momentum and accepting it as
that's just the way it is?
When will we heal and protect the foundations of life, and move
in the ways God has set us up to thrive?
        Progress for what, and at what cost?

JENNY FOOTLE

CHAPTER THREE:

HUMAN TRAFFICKING

IF ONLY

She should have been concerned
When we spent so much time together,
But she never asked what we did.
She should've been concerned when
I stopped using a loofah, and just
Started using my hands.
Or maybe that my cousin liked to hang out with me,
Not my brother, and not my sister, who was closer to his age.
Did you notice that I got my first
Pair of heels when I was 6,
Or that later my dad taught me how to walk in them,
That I was maybe 11 when I asked for my first thong?
I did.

You should have been concerned when
I was able to buy new clothes and shoes,
But I didn't have an allowance or
A job.
Did you wonder why I was gone,
Where I went, or what happened?

Because you never asked me.
       Do you want to know?

THROUGH

So I'm writing this on the wall,
People are supposed to see it there.
You tap on the window because you see me
　　　But I've locked the door.
The door you never knocked on with courtesy
　　　The one that never stopped you until now.
I'm not looking through your façade anymore.
　　　They are looking at mine.
Go ahead, spend all your time covering it with makeup
　　　Beads of sweat will roll down and make it clear in the
heat of the moment.

Here in my moment with them
　　　I'll put on lipstick, leave a mark on their cheek
　　　　　And take off clothes, leaving a mark on their
　　　minds.
Despite your persistence you could never join them
　　　To see who they see
　　　　　When they look at me.
Because in this distance we have strategically placed between us
　　　I have gone without you
　　　　　Into a "they" you'll never see through your
façade.

HOW TO GET TRAFFICKED

Look normal.
No really, don't dress like a hoe.
People watch out for slutty girls;
"Gotta keep an eye on that one."
They don't slip under the radar.
Normal girls do.

Don't have close friends.
Friends that if you leave the party early, they'll keep partying once you leave.
Friends that invite you over for a good time, but will never call you in a low time,
You won't call either.
So when someone you don't really know doesn't interact with anyone else in you life --
Your secret really is their secret,
And they won't check in on you tomorrow to remind you of the pain you were in.

Sincerely be addicted to letting go.
Commitment is your issue.
That's why you can leave.
That's why you don't have a boyfriend,
Or close friends.
You write a journal every day for years and once someone reads it, you stop completely,
And no, you don't want to talk to them about what they read,
Let it go.
You write a chapter book in Word, and 12 pages in at 12pt font, single spaced,
Someone tells you you're no good at writing and it's not a real career and to stop before you're a burden on society ---

You delete it completely.
Without backing it up.
And you don't try again, nor do you cling to that person for your
future.
You let it all go.
So when you see something crazy
Or do something reckless,
You don't feel the need to tell that non-existent supportive
person or those close friends…
You just let it go.

Avoid drama like the plague.
That's how people get drugged.
That's how people get chained to beds.
Instead you get in the car, you don't ask where you're going --
It's not where you came from and that's what matters.
You don't whine, you don't have to talk about it, or compare
notes with the other girls.
You don't demand pot -- they'll give you that, <u>plus</u> pills.
And when you board that plane,
Do not look nervous.
20+ other people are doing it --
Boarding the plane,
But also being trafficked.

Lastly, tell white lies,
Half truths.
Yes I was out with school friends
(one of them goes to school)
Yes I stayed at her house
(that's where I said I was going, I stayed for a couple hours)

And when they have a bad feeling about some of your friends,
Remind them that Jesus didn't hang out with the righteous.
Then let it go,
Write it off as drama,

Know you won't get close to those friends,
And act normal
(you didn't say Jesus hung out with "the other women")
That would give them a big hint --
Don't do that.

GAMES

It's just a game they said
Kids experiment
>But it's different when her dad taught her the game
>She's playing with me now.

Pretend it's a lollipop
You just suck on it until stuff comes out
You like lollipops right? You can't turn one down right?
Don't you like to play pretend?

To me sex is like scrabble
It's just something fun you do with friends
It's not a big deal, it's just like playing board games, but more
fun.
I told my first real boyfriend.

"Let's play a little game"
They said in the movie, to get her out of trouble without freaking
out.
"Let's play a little game"
He said in the movie, to freak her out before killing her.

I don't like to play games.

"I don't like this game"
I thought as he made me touch the cold cement floor while he
fucked me from behind.

"I don't like this game"
I thought while being kept naked outside in the August Arizona
sun.

"I don't like this game"

I thought when they dragged me uphill at dusk in the woods,
shoved me down on a tree and demanded I remove my clothes.

"I don't like this game"
Sitting in a dark room with a killer repeating over and over, "I'm
not what I do"

"I don't like this game"
I think when someone bold face tells me "I don't know what
you're talking about"
When someone tells me "you like this don't you"
Or "I think you should ask God what you did"
Or "You know what you did"

"I don't like this game"
With fencing wire around my neck
As they tell me about chickens with their head cut off

"I don't like this game"
It will only hurt a little
Soon it will be over
You'll get over it
They might miss you, but they'll get over it
Do they even know where you are?
Do you even know where you are?

You're a big girl, figure it out.
If you can do this, then you can do that.
What's one more?
Who cares?
It doesn't matter.
What's the magic word?
Only if you can find it…

I don't like games. I don't want to play. I want to know.

I want to just be. I don't want to try to answer. And I definitely don't want to guess.

NO WORDS

So odd, and ironic, using words to address the issue of people
being manipulative by not using their words…

There's the obvious:
"I never said I hate them."
But you talk about them as if you do…

There's the twisted:
"I'm not angry, there's nothing wrong."
But it's only short, terse replies, or yelling when they engage…

There's the deep:
They never said they're disappointed,
But ever since the incident they push you
Harder than the others.

There's the dark:
They never said they reject you,
But moving you out of sight,
Giving you up for slave labor…
Multiple times, giving you to a man in India, taking your identity
card…

There's straight up cruel:
When you're talking they use their words…
"Did you hear something?"

There's the nothing:
No response, no eye contact, no body language,
Nothing to go off of but the voices in your head.

There's the invalidation:
He didn't say that

You can't jump to conclusions
I'm sure they didn't mean it that way
You're making too big of a deal
It's not as bad as you think
Think of all they've done for you
Don't take it personally
Did they actually tell you that?

But there's love songs about saying it best when you say nothing
at all…

Consent is sexy
Communication is sexier

A lack of words or carefully crafted words does not equate to no
message.
And mean it or not, you sent the message loud and clear
And I responded.

MIXED MESSAGES

Keep your chin up
　　　But your head down
Look me in the eye when I'm talking to you
　　　And avert them at all other times
I want you around
　　　But don't talk to me
You're useful to have around,
　　　But not wanted to be around
Where have you been,
　　　And why are you still here

I'll sleep with you,
　　　And you better be gone by morning…
He had sex with me but I didn't want it
　　　That's rape by the way.
And oh by the way,
　　　You can't win.

Really, we don't know what to do with you
So we'll put you to work,
Move you around,
Like a piece of decoration.

Maybe we'll hang laundry on it,
Use it as a doorstop,
But isn't this a nice piece?

I guess we'll keep it,
Maybe put it in the shed for a while,
Pull it out when people come over.

It's getting a little dull,
Maybe we should clean it up,

Hit it with a hammer so it stands up straighter.
Not too hard,
Don't want to leave any marks.

Yeah that'll do for now.
Until next time.
Are you ready to go?
          Where should we put it this time?
I think we can just leave it,
We can find it later if we need it.

ALL IN ONE, IT ADDS UP, ACCUMULATED

First there was the glass bottle.
Then all the bodies and faces of men from work.
Then I'm sitting on concrete ground close to a brick wall.
The yellow letters
I still stare at them and can't make out what it means.
Him slamming my head down,
Another bending me backwards and suffocating me, another
shoving himself into my butt
All on that same disgusting couch.

The purple finger lines on my breasts days, a week later.
Wondering if on the 3rd day out
I should still go to the hospital and report it.
Looking at myself topless in the mirror.
His blonde, balding hair, glasses, large pale flabby hairy belly
On my small, tan, fit, frame.
The empty room,
Cold and plain with a bland but clean-ish bed
In my pimp's "uncle's" house,
Bending over with my hands on the floor
Because my hands had to touch the concrete floor.

"It's like a lollipop, you just lick it."
So many showers.
So much blood.
Dry throat, did I ever attempt to scream anyway?
Still shaking on the floor
Next to his big comforting thigh.
Kissing him goodbye.
There it goes:

I screamed, from a nightmare.
He came in mad. I apologized.

Still the back of my head hit the wall, he came down on my
wrists, shoved into my knees, shaking me.

Am I living a lie?
What's real or "that bad."
What's just me making it worse?

Me twisting my body/thighs when with the man I love
Snapping back into a flashback like acid in my spinal cord.
Him holding me by my wrists -- me struggling, trying to tame
my facial expression.
Looking away: telling him I freak out if you touch my wrists,
Telling him I'd been raped. Looking down.

Dark, warm, streaming but not noticing, so numb in and out
In jeans, a bar of soap, water
Beating me for over an hour,
Still I get off the dirty tile before I feel clean.

Too small to lay down and drown in the next shower
Still tried.
Red, red, blotchy, uneven, scraped beyond scrubbing
Shower.

"I've got to make this one quicker,
I can't have bruises this time."
Teacher sitting across from me in my own room,
Placing hands on the finger bruise outlines still on my arms and
wrists.
Fail.

Cottage cheese ceiling -- for hours.
Slanted pavement.
Going back.
Rain. Always rain. So much rain.
Grabbing me from behind. Sidewalk curb. "No." "Please no."

"You like that bitch?" Whispers from my shoulder, the blind
side.

Fast breathing -- in class.
Bleeding for months.
Infections.
Over 30 I can name, trying to stay under 100 men.
Wavy hair, converse sticking out of the bathtub
I'm not coming out.
Bullet hole in my window.
Knife, red carpet, in the middle, in the dark.
Edge of the field, barbed wire fence at night.
Scar under my breast.

Shaking scared.
Kit kat oven mit.
Waking up knowing someone else clothed you.
Driving with my braid slammed in the back door.
So much pain, still not enough tears.

LACK THEREOF

Embracing that you're a terrible person
People who need drugs feel so strongly
They can't take it
Or they're so numb they can't resist
The desire to feel something.
Then there's a whole other level
A lack of consciousness
You don't actually need the drugs,
They're just fun.

Then you smile, and they don't ask questions
They know you're playing a different game.
          you're on a whole other level.
Years later when you have your life together,
Full time job, husband, car, apartment…
The psychologist wants to put you on antipsychotics
She tells you it's okay,
you're not psychotic,
don't take it the wrong way
You smile again.
You haven't even told her half of your disturbances.

You outsmart your pimp
Really you've out-crazy-ed him.
Your friends leave you.
You decide to be nice and let them go.
After working in the industry for years
You decide to have fun,
Do someone your own age,
Collect articles of clothing
As you collect V cards,
Later when your judgy friends steal your clothes
You smile, they were never yours,

If only she knew…
Oh well, I guess that leaves me with only short shorts now.
Thanks.

It's hearing gunshots and not wondering what happened.
It's sleeping in a bed while
Someone has sex next to you.
And waking up refreshed.
It's not keeping count.
It's not caring as long as they don't know.
It's not showering for days after.
It's loving Kid Rock's So Hott, Buckcherry's Crazy Bitch,
LMFAO's Don't Trust Me
It's not caring about the word love,
Definitely never using it -- don't want someone to get the wrong
idea.
It's hitchhiking as an attractive young female.
It's always going alone, looking like a knockout
It's answering the door naked
It's doing the work sober,
So you can say it's your choice.
It's deception at its finest
Pure crazy
Pure reckless
Pure survival

THE CAPTURED

It's eating at your heart
It's tearing you apart
And yet you sit
There and let it take over.
You've tried and you still are
But it's hard.
Had you not tried in the first place,
It wouldn't be this bad.
It wouldn't be like this.
It could be your fault.
But it's hollow
You're empty
And trapped.
They'll find you and kill you
You're a project not a person.
It's your job to improve
They'll tell you how, but won't help you.
Too bad isn't it?
Too bad.

FORGET ME

You know you want to
You know you want to look me in the eye
And tell me you don't have a damn clue who the hell I am
That you've never seen me
But you can't

No matter where you go
No matter how much you change
It'll find you, me that is
It's comin' back, my memory that is
But I ain't lookin for you
I got too much of you last time
No, you got somethin' of mine

You want to forget me
But you took a chunk of who I am
You want to bury it
But I'm still breathin'
Just tell me where you put it
Forget it, it's too late to give it back.

There ain't enough of me left to make a person
But you, you got more than one person,
More than one person can handle
So you're stuck, adding another layer of mud
Every time it rains.

You'll try real hard
You'll try real hard to leave me out
Of all your conversations, all your lives, even all them lies

Though when I see you
You'll give me exactly what I want

What you wish you could forget
Is me.

BENEATH

She joked she could fit 5 dead bodies in her trunk
But actually she buried it

A shovel twice her size
Ground too hard to run a plow through
Taught to do as she's told
Not to protest
To speak up is to speak against, to disrespect, to be trouble
So she buried it

Asking for water on a hot day
They watered the ground under her feet instead
And buried it.

She's not to be trusted around others, can't have the privilege of
sitting in service
But everyone must go to church,
Even it it's into the basement
They buried it.

No better than a tool, except you have to feed it, but you even
have to feed a truck oil,
So under the porch with 5 crackers
They buried it.

Secure in the back of her parents' car,
Surrounded by missed stuffed animals,
Away from those people, she was so grateful
She buried it.

Comforting herself when she was alone,
Of all the places she'd been,
Of all the people she'd been,

Telling herself she's not there now
She buried it.

Handed more drugs if she looked troubled
She buried it

Told to only think about it on her break
She buried it

The evidence it happened, in a bag under her desk
She buried it

Letting go of her "stupid" dreams
She buried it

Jesus forgave them, so
She buried it

They didn't know what they really did
And time after time,
She buried that too.

****
That's a lot of digging
Deep holes
Buried deep
But even the earth rejects vile things
And when they resurface
It's always much uglier
Creepy, scary, no one wants to deal with it
But you have to,
Or it will pollute the environment

Sometimes, some things
She buried it
But they weren't bad, and she wants it back

But she doesn't know where to find it
Or how to access it

So I guess she'll be digging
Deep holes
Buried deep
She'll come out alive
A little dirty, but it's okay
She won't bury herself
Anymore

WALK AWAY

The things you forget
Or maybe the things you didn't know then
I thought he was there for me
But there was consequences if I didn't do what he wanted
Only there for me when I woke up
Only there to use me
When I wasn't conscious
When I wasn't fighting
Only complying
When I had no choice

You can always walk away
Until you have no where better to go
Until they're the ones glad to have you around
Until they offer you better…
Offer you "the life"
Until they drug you

But you walked through the door
So you made the choice
And you know what they say,
You pay the price
With your life, with your mind, with your body
How much longer will I pay for this
With my mind
My health
My finances

You can always walk away
But sometimes all you can do is look away
I looked away
From him, from them, from my own pain,
        From my heart, my life

I couldn't walk away…

Now I don't close my eyes
I'm always looking
Looking out for her, for them, for my own pain, for my heart, my
life
I don't live the nightmare anymore
But oh if I close my eyes
I couldn't look away…

Could you? Look away?
From her, from him, from them, from our pain,
        From our hearts, our lives
You can always walk away,
Isn't that what you tell us?
What if you didn't walk away…

We could.

If you didn't look away, so we could.
Could you keep watch for a while, step in for a while…
So we can rest, stop running
And walk free

HAND MADE

I am handmade, carefully crafted by His hand.
He sent me into this world so I might make it as beautiful as I
am.
But with tears in His eyes, He watched me become broken and
abused.
Many were to blame, but none were accused.
Oh how it hurt the Maker to see His creation suffer, and with a
pain in his heart,
He watched me glue myself back together over time, which I
guess makes me plastic in a way,
But that is the result of not asking to be helped with the stitching.
I handed Him the glue,
But He started to paint, brilliant colors of his great love,
Making me as bright as the sunshine above.
Because needles hurt, tears stain, and that's why God wants you
whole again.

CHAPTER FOUR:

TRAUMA

THROUGH

So I'm writing this on the wall,
People are supposed to see it there.
Those clouds the sky leaves between us,
Don't you know they always bring the rain?
Strategically place the tile so it will lay down all right
      Foundations buckle under pressure eventually

Spend all your time covering it with makeup
      Beads of sweat will roll down and make it clear in the
heat of the moment
You tap on the window because you want to be seen
      Doorbells rarely work anymore and no one ever knocks
Put on lipstick, leave a mark on their cheek
      Take off clothes, leave a mark on their minds
Grass grows green, but the roots stay brown
      They're planted in dirt and only grow deeper down.
The only way to draw a well rounded figure
      Is to make it shady around the edges.

      Help! right? Isn't that what I'm supposed to scream?
No, silence; like you my voice is gone,
Hopefully it'll change for the both of us when I pass on.

On passing, I'm about to miss the train again.
It only runs on track(s).
If you see me, do turn away.
      And hope the sun shines on a different day.

LEFT

You left your keys on the table
By the chair with the faded seat
Still warm

From where you left

The heavy door wide open
Now with a dent in the wall
From the knob
          Jarred by sweaty smears

of your hands

That left a mark
On my face
Is the look of pain, confusion

You left me with
              them.

Lying still in the bed you tucked them into
They are looking to me for answers
              you didn't leave with me.

PERMANENT DAMAGE

I clench in stillness every time I hear a door struggling to open,
or close.
Doors whose frames have been offset
Shaken by tiny earthquakes.
I feel them.
But other people are shocked to find out that they occur, they
have to hear about it on the tv or radio before they believe it.
And by then it's just an interesting fact.
I think I'm the only one who's put two and two together that the
house frames are off
Because of these tiny shakes and tremors
That no one feels but me.
But I'm not crazy,
It's like how someone who's broken a bone knows it's gonna
rain,
They know because they feel the pain
Again. Where they were once broken.
I feel it too, when the door frame resists.

BLUE JEANS

How plain and simple they appear
Plain Jean blue
Simply slide them on and there you go!
Literally.

Gone! See you later

Today? Tomorrow? Tonight? Too late.
We are going somewhere
Who knows where or when, they are carrying me away.
They hug my legs closely and never let go
Trustworthy.

Somewhere they will have to loosen up and get off me!
Somewhere!
Something will cause them pain and they will let me know?
Some thing?
Sometime they will have to calm down and stop showing off.
Some time.

Until that time comes
We will have the time of our lives
Time only leads to death.
Death no longer scares us, though
Death has been biting at our heels
Before we had heals to bite.

We don't fear separation
Because when we do
They lay there, never quite folding the same way

Waiting, worn to a fuzz that glows
The sunlight comes through the same window that reveals

Where you could be instead of where you are.
Give in, you know you want to.

Look closer to every detailed thread,
The blue explodes in shades
The way they curve,
How do all the lines go straight down?
They are held together by golden strings
Built to last through golden years of brilliance
Built to outlast me.

DREAM BREACH

I had a dream last night that I did not like.
In fact, I woke up from it
and I made quite a commotion. But the warm body beside me
remained on my lofted bed so either
it wasn't that bad or he got me before
the edge got him. Unfortunately
It followed the same pattern as all the others.
This one started at the beginning. It was raining but I
parked my car a few blocks away anyway,
It was habit. Jeans, Converse, football style shirt,
my favorite one:
maroon with gold numbers. And yes,
despite the Tulsa July heat of the night
 I did wear jeans. Never would I wear a skirt, I wasn't that girl.
But now I wonder if it would have been less harsh
if I was wearing one
but I know I would question it like I'm questioning my jeans
now.

I was walking from my car, phoneless, putting my car key
in my pocket, putting my ID there too.
Looking both ways to cross the street, crossing quickly,
raining harder. Going down the sidewalk
towards the club, my parents thinking I'm in Missouri.
For once no ecstasy in my system, no speed,
steps in the right direction. Drunk man passes and says
something I pass off.
Keep walking. Two men on my sidewalk, why are so many
people
leaving my destination? One bumps me, says he's sorry,
the other asks me a question, arms entrap mine from behind,
boy in front of me – his body now very close to mine, more
bodies,

arms tighten behind me so much I can only look down. Now we're walking
all together, step down off the sidewalk, so much darkness in the night.
I awake, struggling.

DREAM BREACH 2

I had a dream last night that I did not like.
I woke and made somewhat of a commotion. But the warm
body beside me remained on my lofted bed.
Unfortunately the dream followed
the same memory as all the others.
The dream started at the beginning. It was raining but I
parked my car a few blocks away anyway. And yes,
despite the Tulsa July heat of the night
I did wear jeans. I wasn't the kind of girl who wears flashy
skirts.
But now I wonder if it would have been less harsh
if I was wearing a skirt
but I know either way I would question my choices
as if I could have prepared for what transpired that night.

I was walking from my car, putting my key
in my pocket, along with my ID.
Looking both ways to cross the street, crossing quickly,
raining harder. Going down the sidewalk.
No one knew I was there.
Drunk man passes and says something I dismiss.
Keep walking. Two men on my sidewalk, why are so many
people
leaving? One bumps me, says he's sorry,
the other asks me a question, arms entrap mine from behind,
boy in front of me – his body now very close to mine, more
bodies,
then arms tighten behind me so much I can only look down. Now
we're walking
all together, step down off the sidewalk, so much darkness in the
night.

FIGHT, FLIGHT, FREEZE, AND ⋯

At first you learn about fight or flight,
Then it happens to you
After it percolates in your mind
What you did and didn't do,
They tell you about "freeze"

Eventually you find solidarity in knowing your reaction is legit
and not just you…
But then these situations keep happening,

Now you're cognisant,

Trying to fight
Then realizing that only hurts more.
Trying to flee but getting stuck,
You're mentally aware --
But obviously not frozen.

So what's next?

Make it easy,
Please them,
The sooner they get what the want,
The sooner you're off the hook.

You know it wasn't consensual,
But they text you the next day,
"I had a great time last night."

Now what.

PTSD TRASH

It's hard to believe that the trash
Will no longer be an issue
When it keeps accumulating,
And it's even harder when
You have to go home every day
To the cat who made the mess
In the house,
Especially because it's a repeat
Offender,
It's hard justifying that it gets attention
Time on your lap.

NOT ABOUT TRAUMA

I won't write about what it's like to live with trauma.
Know why? Because I'm a survivor!
You wake up in the morning and think to yourself,

Damn! I slept good, I only woke up twice.
I may have been sweaty, but I didn't scream!
Yep. It's gonna be a good day.

that alley you walk past at 4:30am may look like the one you
were raped in,
but hey, it's not the same one --
you packed up your whole life and moved ten hours away, now
thirteen hours,
and besides, you always walk on the other side of the street
anyway.

You might feel short on breath every now and then passing it,
But congrats survivor, you made it!
And you probably can't breathe because you're walking fast,
Not because you're female, alone, and it's dark outside,
But because you don't waste time, and you're walking downhill.

So many reasons why you're walking fast,
breathing hard... because you're just that determined to punch in
the time clock.
It's okay that you zoned out folding towels,
The scene in your mind that just paralyzed you,
Aren't you glad that's behind you!
And no one is actually behind you, just a wall.
Besides, people commonly zone out at that time in the morning...
at least you weren't driving!

Count your blessings, God has spared your life once more, and aren't you glad you still have your mind about you to think of all these things?

...It's only 7am...

NORMAL

Normal is relative
Nice people say there is no such thing as normal… but in
America,

Normal is finishing high school
Going to the movies with someone you love
Having one friend obsessed with pizza
Having a favorite color.

Owning clothes you picked out for you --
not work, not for him, not for them, not for culture --
at least a week's worth --
just because, forget them.

Normal is getting to be you, more often than not
-- you don't get paid enough to act.
Normal is getting cake on your birthday.
Normal is going to bed, to sleep, every night.
Normal is a teen or twenty something enjoying an outdoor
concert with friends.
Normal is being around people who know you, at least one you'd
call friend.

Giving kindness, without expecting a return.
Having friends, going out with said friends.
Enjoying sunshine, being thankful for rain.

Drinking one without having too many.
Being able to make a salad,
Making mac n cheese
Knowing there's a difference between a dry cup and a wet cup.

Owning a coat

Owning boots
Not owning hand-me-down underwear!
Brushing your teeth daily
Eating more than one meal a day.
Not sleeping in your car
Having a job as an adult.

Having a sense of value, without a price tag, or thinking you're a
gift to the world.
Normal is going outside on a nice day, and staying in when it's
not.
Normal is having seen a doctor in the last 5 years. Updating your
glasses, knowing you have insurance.

Normal is having someone you can tell hard things to.
Normal is feeling at home, in your home.
What's not normal -- finding peace, maybe even excitement --
about being normal.
Being able to say I love you.

CONSCIOUS

I have a conscience.
I mean, I didn't
But I'm growing
Becoming more human
More aware
Actually caring
      About me.

First it starts with seeing it
      For what it is
Then speaking it, to a journal, in art, to a friend
      Without the self blame.
      Without the "buts"
            I didn't want it but
            I didn't think ___ but
            I said no but
You do the work, you roll your shoulders back, you speak about
it plainly, as if the buts aren't even acceptable to you.

Eventually it becomes a response
Your brain doesn't have to tell you
Your body knows
You can't believe the buts, you can't believe "it"

You feel like the room is spinning
You feel like you're going to throw up
You can't go about your business as if it didn't happen.
You lose your breath
Your concentration
You have to say something
You lose your ability to not care
You have a conscience.

****

And it's beautiful. It's real.
You're alive. You're healthy.
It's good to feel deeply.

It's not good to not care,
To move on and shrug off bad things,
To see and experience things and never expose the darkness.
It's inhumane, to you,
To those you choose not to see.

It's survival, it's not a place to live.
Your conscious speaks;
You're beautiful, real, alive, healthy.
Let it speak, and don't be afraid to let it be loud.
Love it, accept it.

THE REAL DEAL

It didn't bother me when you told me the things you hate about me.
But I didn't respond when you said you couldn't stop watching my videos.
[I'm programmed not to respond to hate
It's either a waste of energy, incites more hate,
Or is your backwards way of saying you love me.
It's not threatening, it's how some people just are.
I blow it off so I don't blow up later and look like the fuel,
Justifying your hate…
But when you said I was more adorable,
Or got shyly excited to see me twice in one week…
Now I'm scared.]

I can be feisty and defend my career choices when you question them.
But I struggle to respond to or acknowledge your apologies for touching me inappropriately.
[After all, I am a woman, I'm used to men questioning my worth,
And the world telling me I'm not paid enough,
But they never tell you how to fix it.
I rebuttal with generosity.
But the body, my body, a woman's body -- price tags and values…
And if I let you feel guilty,
Or acknowledge you did something wrong --
My value goes down,
My power shifts,
And you slowly stop giving me what I need,
Because you can't have what you want.
Until I'm done taking from you,
I'll be silent.
Even then I'll be quiet -- I might need more…

One day I'll realize I'm enough and I don't need what you
offer…
But until then…
I'll tell you no, I'll play with fire,
Wondering when I'll meet a man who won't ask me what I'm
worth,
Or tell me with his actions.]

CONVERSATION WITH MY BODY

I sat with you
But you're not here
I keep looking at you, expectantly
But still nothing
I should just get up and leave you
Walk away and give up, stop trying
But you catch me just enough
You shift and I wonder what you'll do next
Did I get somewhere? Was that a response to me?
Or you're just… okay. You're just, there. Okay

So I finally ask, what would you like to do today?
Since you obviously don't like my ideas
You can read my mind, and you're not enthused
At least you're responding
"I want to be"

CHAPTER FIVE:

A LITTLE BIT OF

EVERYTHING

THAT F WORD

Females.
Hott, ugly, damn smart or mind-blowingly dumb.
Elicit the 1 word sentence:
Fuck.

Yep, that's what they come down to
Whether they come to you
Or you cum for them

Fe... iron males
God didn't make us with
Body parts that cripple us in one blow.
No, we can show off our parts that stick out and it's appreciated,
Unlike males, no one wants to see that.

And I think it might hurt worse
to be kicked in the shins than an
onslaught to my genitals.
Which works out because less people/men are interested in
assaulting your shins.
Fuck.

Females
A lot like bombs
Often shiny, well polished,
At least the cartoon versions
Some look more like alarm clocks
You only wish the others would
warn you when time's up.
Some are strapped to guys,
who are holier than thou, yet dream of 10,000 virgins more than
meeting God.
Fuck.

Some blow when they're plugged in,
Added to the right mix,
Or given too much shit.
Then there's those who just need to be shaken up.
Some will go down with the ship,
and wait.

Many are left to the green grass
and abandoned in a field because so many
blew up around them,
they're feared, those are often the ones who've buried their
power,
but you walk lightly
Knowing they're out there, just waiting.
Fuck.

Life starts with the female... and the famous last word?

Sometimes it feels like it's just a matter of who fucks who up first. So you might as well get on with it, we're *all* waiting.

Oh yea, there really is no better word...

ENTER THROUGH AN EXIT

Happiness is a smile I wear
When I want you to love me.

Hurt is a burden I bear
From all that surrounds me.

Love is a gift that cannot be found.
Anger is a root that grows deep in the ground.

My mind reels and my head spins.
But your patience is always wearing thin.

My mind deceives me and so do you.
Conflict is a double-edged sword you pulled me through.

Why are you going back there where I've been.
You're wading in dirt clear up to your chin.

We can end this, we can mend this.
But you'll let it rot, just like you made me.

Now go pick a daisy, and do not stray too far.
Beauty is near and you're not up to par.

THE THINGS THAT STICK

My green card was pink!
I had to sew her breast back on.
I thought I was dying, so I just layed down so as not to disturb anyone.
The text read "She's lost downtown and has blood all over her."
　　　But when we brought her home, I gave her a bath, and she put on white pants.
She was 9, she died in my arms, in the middle of an intersection, in the middle of the day.
The brick was still inside her when they brought her to the hospital.
I know someone who can put a pop can up their vagina without denting it – said a 6th grader.
I'm as wonder bread as it gets, but I've been toasted.
You know, they were some of the nicest people!
　　　-said about porn stars by Wonder Bread
I have 4 kids, I'm 33.
I have 3, my oldest is 22, I was maybe 14.
Because jail wasn't punishment enough.
"They see us too," said the man acting as a demon
"We can't find you," the cop that called 10 minutes after I called saying I was being attacked.

TRY AGAIN TRY SOMEONE ELSE

Yep. I loved it. It did feel great.
He was bored or done with you.
Someone dropped the ball.
No worries, I got it.
You don't.

Are you a people pleaser?
Me too.

The difference? You need them to like you.
I just want them to be happy, give them the boost to rebound, let
'em know they still got it, and can be loved, make someone
smile.
You please so they'll stay, so they can't live without you, so they
think you're invaluable.

Bitch please, I know my value, bout time you discovered yours
and stopped askin' people for it.

F*MALES

Remind me why are we doing this
Really, whose damn idea was it
Play nice, yea right.
Isn't that sexist?
Telling me I have to make friends with and have more female friends...

Because I'm female
I'm full blown female
I think I have enough female in my life -- It is the story of my life.

"Men only talk to women because they want to think they can have sex with you."
Thank you, dear husband.
"You can be a bitch because you're pretty and people will still like you."
Thank you, dear sister.

Anybody else?
C'mon, you know you secretly need to hate someone or
Judge them so much there is no room for hate left.

DESERT OVER GREEN PASTURES

It's always raining…
But it's never raining.
Less than 1 inch for the entire year
It's July.
Where I came from
It rained that night
When I went back
It poured
Where I went, half to get away,
It didn't rain.
Only when I tried to go,
Did it storm.
So I went home
And it froze.
But I came out here
And there hasn't been a drop of rain,
Only blazing heat and
Cracked, but hard ground.
The sun comes early and stays even later.
And I am finally fulfilled.

THE SIMPLICITY OF DOING ··· OR NOT DOING

It's that easy -- just don't.
Don't spend your money, don't go out to get it, don't even call
that person -- just don't.
Feeling jittery? Contacting them will also make you jittery.
You're going to be like this either way, so just don't. It's actually
easier to not.

Feel like you can't? Just do.

Don't swallow all the steps at once, don't take them all in at
once.
Stairs, steps, were made to be taken one at a time.
How dumb would you look if you tried to jump multiple stairs at
once, even just two at once -- people would look at you like --
"Why?"
You fill out the application, you wait, you call, you keep going,
they tell you what comes next, and you take that step.

Can't get out of bed in the morning? Just do.
Can't fathom going to work? Just go.
Don't want to make that call? Just do.

It all has an end, including how long you can stay in bed.

If you don't you lose
So if you want to lose that habit, weight, friend - then don't
But if you don't want to lose that shorter commute, your job, or
that relationship, then do, just do.
You know what the minimal effort is, and you know maybe one
step above that -- so <u>do</u>…
What you want.

ONE FOR US

The fact that I never slept with you
Is the greatest satisfaction
You had to tear me down, or try,
I was the one person who didn't
Give you everything you wanted
Nor was I terribly impressed by
You.

You yelled, and kicked, and hit, and stifled
But I said no.
No you cannot have me
No I will not be yours
No you're not the best
And yes there is <u>much</u> better
Oh, and no, you cannot stay in my life
I said no

PROGRESS

Taking the sleeping bag out of the trunk
And the change of clothes
And the restraining order.

Only packing snacks if I know I'll need them
Not because I don't know what my day will hold.

Buying coffee if I forget it
or just because…
Instead of going without.

Leaving work early when I can
Instead of looking for something to do to get more time.

Going on a week long vacation
Instead of 3 nights
Over a weekend.

Sitting in silence
Instead of having to move, read, talk, or listen.

Not having a time or monetary budget
On being in relationship

Doing what I want
Without caring what others expect
Even when I'm alone.

Being grateful for the experience
Instead of distraught over failure

Acknowledging all the contributors
Owning my responsibility

No more

My life is about me
Not for anyone else
Contributing, not control

Loving
Regardless of the outcome
Without regret

BUT GOD

I may not be smarter,
      But I learned more.

I may not make the grade,
      But I enjoyed the subject.

I may not do all the moves perfect,
      But I never get tired of the way it feels.

There are many things I can do even if
      I am out done.

To a few things, I gave my all
      And never won.

I may not know if I'll pass the test or make the mark,
      But I'll try and barely fail and keep getting up to go
again.
But I guess it's easy for me to risk it all when there's no way to
play it safe,
      No safety net, no sure thing, no comfort zone.
You may have a fall back plan,
      Or at least a place to land, day by day.
You may be good looking and wanted for your skills.

But I live, I really live.
I don't need a drug to have a good time.
I will dance the night away and not stop when I sweat.
I will go for it, knowing that your fear is all you really have to
lose.
I smile when the sun comes up instead of hiding from another
day.

I don't wonder what people really think, because I know the One
who cares.

He'll always be with me whether
	I live up to standards or let you down.
He will laugh with me in the dark
	To protect me from thoughts.
He talks to me even when he doesn't
	Expect something from me.
He loves me even as he watches
	Me hurt him.
And I love Him, always, and we're together through it all.
And we live, He really does.

THE AFTERMATH

Facing him, facing her, facing yourself
The roll over, the lingering pain
But you have to get up

COMPASSION

Compassion for myself
    For how it affected me
    For how I reacted
    For the patterns I created
Compassion instead of combat
    Combatting myself
    Being annoyed at how much it affected me
    Surprised at how I reacted
Only on a mission to unravel the patterns
    Fix myself
    Instead of focusing on healing.
Healing is not the act of fixing yourself.
Healing is finding compassion
Foremost for yourself.

JESUS LOVES ME

Jesus loves me
This, I know.
For my life experience tells me so
Every little broken piece of my heart, to him belongs
The perpetrators are weak,
But God,
is strong.

Yes Jesus loves me.
Yes, the king of heaven loves me.
Yes, indeed I am loved
The spirit that lives within me, and will never leave me,
        Tells me so.

www.ingramcontent.com/pod-product-compliance
Lightning Source LLC
Chambersburg PA
CBHW072021150726
47999CB00002B/746